A Priest & His Dog

A Priest & His Dog

THE TALE OF TATI

BY MALACHI MARTIN

Illustrations by Jerome Atherholt

Foreword by Wolfgang Smith

Angelico Press

First published in the USA
by Angelico Press 2020

For information, address:
Angelico Press, Ltd.
169 Monitor St.
Brooklyn, NY 11222
www.angelicopress.com

ppr 978-1-62138-660-5
cloth 978-1-62138-661-2
ebook 978-1-62138-662-9

Book and cover design
by Michael Schrauzer
Cover image: Jerome Atherholt

FOREWORD

THEA AND I DID NOT KNOW THIS would be the last meeting with our precious friend; and just as our taxi was ready to leave for the airport, Malachi Martin handed me a large manila envelope. When I opened it after we were airborne, I found that it contained the story of a friendship—of a deep love in fact—between a little Cairn Terrier named Tati and Malachi Martin himself: "No one had ever shown me the love little Tati gave me," he confided to his friends.

I welcome the publication of this one-of-a-kind manuscript from the hand of a literary giant—notwithstanding the fact that it is highly personal, and addressed apparently to a circle of kindred spirits. *The Tale of Tati* is a rare jewel, and a testament, not only to Malachi Martin's genius as a story-teller, but above all to his eminence as a sacerdotal servant of Christ.

It needs first of all to be noted that the story exceeds the established genre of animal tales: for heartwarming and deeply moving though it be, it presupposes a certain "openness" to the supernatural, failing which the most precious insights Malachi Martin conveys will remain undisclosed. Not intended, thus, for readers imbued with the wisdom of the world, it calls for the openness of a child before the mysteries of God, which will ever be "*foolishness to the Greeks*" (1 Cor. 1:23).

We may take it that Malachi Martin looked upon his canine companion not indeed as an "animal" in the customary sense—a judgment-laden concept—but simply as a "creature of God," who as such partakes somewhat of His mystery. And this in itself brings the "supernatural" into the picture, not as something extraneous—something imposed, as it were, from outside—but on the contrary: *as the innermost element of all,* which supports all other constituents of that creature.

But then, if that "innermost element" eludes the sense-based conceptions of the rational mind, by what means or faculty can we know it, to the extent that we do? I believe Malachi Martin would concur that the faculty in question is none other than what mystics call *the heart*; and I think he would agree likewise that the knowledge to which that faculty gives access may rightfully be characterized as *love*: love at its deepest level, that is.

To be sure, this is hardly the place to enter upon reflections of this kind, and I will not pursue the metaphysics beyond this point. Nor do we need to: for whosoever has grasped the crux of what has been stated thus far will readily follow what Malachi Martin has to tell us about his little friend. Nor will he find it hard to empathize with Malachi in his ardent hope that this noble creature may ultimately enter into the eternal Love of God—notwithstanding the fact that her animal soul has been declared "mortal" by theologians of note. Who is ever entitled, after all, to set bounds upon that Love! There are pundits, to be sure, parading their wisdom, who would measure all things in heaven and earth with their vaunted yardsticks: let these modern-day Pharisees be chastened, then, and put to shame by the pure love of a little Cairn Terrier.

It appears that *The Tale of Tati* breaks new ground. Charming and touching as it may be, its true message and prime significance is *spiritual*, having to do ultimately with the mystery of the animal soul, and the possibility of its participation in that supreme blessedness termed "life eternal." The great question is whether that *summum bonum* is attainable for the likes of Tati, as our heart would wish—conceivably with the aid of a human intermediary? While not declaring himself on this issue in explicitly metaphysical or theological terms, it appears that Malachi Martin is in fact weighing in heavily on this long-disputed conundrum: *on the side*, that is, *of his canine friend.*

It follows that, when it comes to *The Tale of Tati*, Malachi Martin's renown as one of the great raconteurs of the twentieth century is insufficient endorsement: we need in addition to know something concerning his credentials as a man of God. We should know, first of all, that Malachi was no stranger to spiritual combat, but a battle-tested soldier of Christ, who had passed through his own "dark night of the soul." That in 1958 he was elevated to a top position in the Vatican, becoming a confidant of Pope John XXIII and Pope Paul VI; that he resigned this coveted appointment in 1965 and made his way to New York, where he arrived penniless to begin his career as the leading historian of the Catholic Church and best-selling author. I might mention that when I met Malachi Martin in 1997, he was supporting 49 indigent acquaintances from the proceeds of his best-sellers, while he himself resided in a room barely large enough for his bed, desk, bookshelves, and a humble altar upon which to say Mass. It had been made available to him by a sympathetic Greek family soon after his arrival in New York: and here is where he wrote his books, carried out his voluminous correspondence bringing solace to countless souls—and yes, lived out the tale you are about to read.

Approach it gently, dear reader, "with folded hands" if you are able: a man of God is baring his heart.

Wolfgang Smith

A Priest & His Dog

THE TALE OF TATI

Malachi B. Martin
116 East 63rd Street
New York City, New York 10021
April 13, 1996

MY DEAR FITZ AND CECILE,

It probably sounded very puzzling to you when I said on the phone that "nobody ever gave me the love little Tati gave me." So, I thought I should somewhat explain myself to you—and incidentally explain myself to myself. For, at the age of 75—supposedly "a very old age" (ha! ha!)—I find that I am devastated, truly devastated interiorly, by the passing on of a little Cairn Terrier who spent all but the first three weeks of her mortal existence of 15 years in my home and in my life. It is this devastation that has made me think and reflect on what she came to mean in my life.

If you had told me when I was, say, thirty—and already had assisted both parents to die rather slow deaths at relatively young ages (Daddy at 64, Mummy at 54; both in the same four months)—that I could be so devastated, I would have laughed. Even if you told me that in 1981 when I had lost the two priestly ikons of my life, brothers Bill and Connie, I would have laughed. The ironic touch to life is that on November 28 of that same year (my sixtieth year) Tati was born in Kansas and registered as a pedigree female #RA733823 by the *American Kennel Club* as a descendent of three full generations of Wheaten dams and sires (with glorious names like Robby Boy of Dalgerry, Rebecca Pandora, Sir Lancelot of Vernon, Bly the Lad of Gergler, Merry Missy Laddieskin, Petula Pandora, and on and on for all 14 of them)!

It was Kakia who brought her home from the Kennel—but she did not pick Tati; Tati had picked her. I was the one who named her Tatiana. That was in honor of my favorite, Tatiana, among the martyred Russian princesses about whom I had been reading that year.

When I look back now, it seems impossible that a little terrier—she was the runt in a litter of seven, mind you—could so establish herself in my life (quite insensibly as far as I was concerned) that only after she passed on would I realize by her absence how prime a place she occupied in all my waking and sleeping hours. I exaggerate not, as you will see, if you read on.

The thing grew naturally, the association, I mean. There was the real puppy-dog period when we house-trained her so that she wouldn't have to be "walked" twice a day in these dirty streets of New York—which she hated anyway for their noise and confusion

and harshness. New York's streets are never benign, never roseate-smiling, never welcoming. They are not homes of beauty. Just, of power. They overawe. And Tati wanted none of them. She always put on the total shivering act every time I took her out in my arms to the groomer and the doctor. She just shook from head to toe, seemingly in every bone and sinew. On the last day of her life, she totally shivered as I carried her to the car.

Once house-training was accomplished—it took about nine months moving her toilet papers inch by inch to a designated place, forever after she would repair to that place for her toiletries, etc. She was summarily trainable, made to be trained. She cottoned on very fast to what was to be done. I have regrets, deep regrets on this point. If I only had known how, I could have taught her so much more that would have facilitated her physical life—like how to drink water; she had a very weak trachea which gave her seven months of hard labor in the last year of her life; that's one example. However, now she is beyond regrets and at great peace.

The exploration of the pre-eminence she occupied at the time of her departure follows from these antecedents. Over time (a short time) and between her 2nd and 5th year she established herself in the household as a functioning part of it. She chose her own armchair: a place in the living room from which, at her ease, she could surveille the front door and elevator, the kitchen, the back door, the living room, my room, KL's room and beyond. Her hearing was fantastic, so she could detect who was coming up from the sound of their voices long before *we* heard them. When the bell at either door rang, she had a certain bark for each one. When the outside bell of the main apartment house door sounded, she sounded off (another kind of bark). When any of the household left, she accompanied them with barks; likewise when they came back. She had different barks for KL, for Genie, for me, for Maria. The day (in her last year of life) when she ceased to bark (her trachea started collapsing, making her breathing very labored), something died in the house, and of course foreboding started. The last time she barked was in a warning to me after a very troublesome telephone call and a brush with the Enemy. Just that once, her head came up, ears pointing, the tail moving, and a bristling growl before and after. She sensed both devils and angels.

She proceeded to routinize me, if I can use that awful word. In the morning, the moment she heard me get up (she slept either in KL's section or my section of the house) she signaled by scratching on the door. Then she needed attention: toiletries, fresh water, and her vitamin tablet. She waited for KL to wake up, then she needed her breakfast. Quite insistently; followed by some activity, usually with one of her air-filled little balls. By that time, the maid (Edna or Esther) arrived. She was off to watch them, return for a visit to me, watch KL, and so into the morning, always active, always circulating between the kitchen, KL's study, my study and the front door. Lunch was a ritual again; she stayed with KL who lunched; then I came and gave her her lunch. Then she frequented my room, sleeping on my bed, scavenging in the kitchen, vigiling on her armchair. When both of us were ordered to take siestas—KL and I—Tati distributed her time between us, sleeping in whichever room. But if there was no siesta, then she came by preference to me, sometimes lying on my floor in the sun (my windows have a southern aspect), or asleep on my bed, or insisting on my attending to her—in various ways: either she had lost her currently favorite ball or pushed it into some inaccessible place (beneath the radiators) so that she forced me to dig it out slowly for her while she waited to pounce on it at the count of 1-2-3; or she wanted to be caressed; or she wanted a biscuit, or, or, or, or. Her inventiveness was truly amazing; I mean a lot of thought and connivance went into this. She was in continual movement because nothing happened that did not call forth her energies: people entering or leaving the neighboring apartment, messenger boys at the back door (special targets), dogs passing by and barking, telephone bells, cooking smells from the kitchen, and so on.

It was during these hours that she initiated her "talking tours" as I called them. In the beginning she just indicated she would like to be picked up, and showed no inclination to get down. In that situation, I started to walk around with her—around the apartment—letting her peek at the street through the opening in the curtains (her interest-span in the street was minimal), craning her neck to watch something she couldn't see from the floor, turning her head to see the ceiling (always on the watch for her feared #1 enemy, flies and mosquitoes and little bugs). As a natural extension of this she used to roll over on her side and eventually her back, paws in the air, eyes wide open, gazing mutely at the passing scene—she saw parts of the furniture and the wall decor she never saw from the floor. Within a short time, she got up into my arms, rolled over and lay there while I walked around slowly, room to room, in detailed progression, I talking all the time about what we did in each room with the names of those who frequented the rooms whom she remembered— KL, self, herself, Edna/Esther, Genie, Tia, Michael, June Meier. During those tours, she would gaze peacefully at the passing scene, moving her head from side to side, occasionally turning to lick my wrist or hand, never showing any sign that she wanted the "talking tour" to end.

This led to another habit of hers played out either on my table where I wrote or on my bed. She would bother me until I lifted her up on my table, then squat down on all fours, back legs spread out, her head lifted and she proceeded to lick my hands and my face, stopped, looked at me intently, then started again. At other times, she would lie on the bed, her eyes half-closed. How she brought it around I don't quite know, but I would crook my arm around her, bury my face in her fur at her neck level and talk—the same sort of talk, but this time about Mass, about the Angels, her Angel and my Angel, about Heaven, Our Lord, Our Lady, Francis of Assisi, the Saints. At one stage, as I talked she would start this low moaning—no growl there, just moaning, her body utterly still. The more I spoke about immortality and Heaven and the Trinity and the Angels, the more she moaned at a higher pitch, but always gentle, always quiet, no strain of protest or pain or anything negative, and pacing herself with my words. It ended with me going back to work at my writing table and Tati lying there for a while, half asleep, until some distraction interrupted her somnolence and silence.

At night, for the years 2–8, she slept on my pillow or on KL's pillow or at the foot of my bed. All those years (2–8), I would be awakened at the same time by Tati, in the morning. She lay on my pillow, looking out over life as if transfixed by some object or sight. Still keeping her eyes fixed on that object, she would bend down and cover my forehead with saliva, warm saliva. When I fell asleep again, she would wait a few minutes, and then go through the same process; until for as many times as it took, she had me completely awake; then we got up and the usual morning rituals were accomplished. Once she was cleaned, fed and satisfied, she lay there while I said Mass and my Rosaries. When KL got up, she attached herself to her, but always noting where I was and if I was eating. She had a principle: if I ate, she should eat. I had all sorts of ruses to avoid eating in front of her. But I couldn't beat or evade her sense of smell.

What I am trying to convey here is that she—as it were automatically and naturally—inserted herself into the life of the household and into my personal life, so that her physical presence and the play of her personality were daily and constantly associated with all I did. Tati was always there everywhere I was. And remember I work at home, and my circadian rhythm is strictly sedentary and at home.

When I had to travel for weeks on end publicizing my books in the years '83–'91, the day I came back, she greeted me in a very characteristic manner: prostrate on the ground, her head bowed to the ground, her eyes closed, her paws splayed out; nothing would do but that I lift her up, hug her, kiss her, she licking me furiously and repeatedly. KL was always jealous in a loving way of Tati's closeness to me.

Tati had such peculiar habits, I always wondered where she got them. Remember that she was taken from her litter-mother at age three weeks and delivered to us. There was no period of training by imitation with any other dog or being. Yet she had those *constant* reactions, and so particular that you wonder how? Why? The prostration I mentioned above is one. It came out also in the presence of babies. When each of Michael's children was born, of a certain age (a couple of months), their mother Sophia brought each child to visit their grandmother (KL). Each time we showed the baby (George or Alexandra) to Tati—we did so by lowering the baby to her level; Tati went into her prostration act, groveling on her belly, legs splayed out, daring only to glance fleetingly at the baby's face, keeping her eyes down and licking the feet of the baby. It really was something. Her behavior at my Mass was also very peculiar, in that sense of peculiar: to lie utterly still and, as it were, attentive, specifically for the duration, and then—once finished—to start her "doggy" behavior; I always found this peculiar.

Her phobias were something else. In the kitchen sink, besides the two faucets (hot and cold) we have a sort of a flexible pipe that pulls out to a length of 2 1/2–3 feet, and by pressing the nozzle you get all the hot or cold water you need in a jet. Tati went crazy every time I took this into my hand, barking violently and jumping and obviously alarmed and distressed. The same reaction of protesting barks, jumping and alarm came when I attempted each evening (having loaded the dishwasher) to pour some of the Calgonite into the little feeder of the dishwasher. The moment I *touched* the box of Calgonite, Tati went into a blue frenzy, barking, jumping, distressed. Her sense of smell and fear of this was so great that, when I waited for her to leave the kitchen with KL, and when they were both at the other end of the house, and when I would then take out the box of Calgonite to put it into the dishwasher; I would just have the box opened when Tati would come back at the double all the way from the den at the other end of the house, barking, jumping, very distressed. We never found out why.

Her existence modified the way I behaved in early mornings and late at night, during broad daylight and during the night. She intervened at moments of great distress for me: when the Devil threw me out of my bed one night in a rage at me, the first thing I knew was Tati's hot breath and affectionate licking, telling me I was alive, that it was all right; I was just on the floor, shaken but okay. In some months prior to my bad fit of pneumonia, Tati, who was sleeping with me during that cold weather, turned a very fixed stare at me one night when the pain in the left-hand side of my chest was bad; she gave me a very fixed and studying gaze, then she proceeded to salivate all over my pyjamas, wetting that part of my chest with this warm liquid, then she turned her back and nestled into my chest. I fell asleep shortly after, and that pain ceased by the morning.

Insensibly, and without my realizing how she effected it, I became very dependent on seeing her, hearing her, feeling her coat, playing with her in her favorite games. I loved the smell of her breath, the varying colors of her coat (steely grey in autumn and winter; apricot and silvery gold in spring and summer). I formed an attachment which for a long time I thought would last forever. When old age beset me myself; and when in her last two years her mortality started to assert itself; then I asked Christ to take her before me because I wanted always to be there for her and never have her lacking.

By now you can see Tati could give me a love and happiness that nobody else could. A small little dog, a terrier, a pedigree terrier, beautiful in her own way, with all the pedigree markings required by her breed—black tips to the ears and paws and tail, delicate snout, who never tired of being with me, who could be with me everywhere, who mirrored the joy of angels and their singular devotion, and above all a little dog who seemingly could transcend the obvious limitations of her canine nature. How could I not become dependent on her? This last point is tremendously important—the transcending power.

There seems to have been definite phases in her life, especially in the last six years of her life, when she achieved self-reflective consciousness; when you could see clearly she was conscious of herself almost saying "I am an I," "I am me," "distinct from you." There is a metaphysical and a supernatural question here.

Metaphysically, she never treated me as her *master*. She treated me as her father, her care-giver, her feeder, her charge. And in those special moments of her "talking tours," and, more particularly during our "moaning" sessions—I always called her "mummy-puppy" plus a lot of other pet names—"lion in winter," "angel of God," etc.—there were intuitive moments when she was obviously straining against the bounds of her canine mortality, moaning and bemoaning, while my spirit kept assuring her that it was okay, that I had spoken to Our Lord Jesus, the Lord of Life, that He would take her gently out of her mortality, that she would be with Him and with me and with her Nona forever. And all this passed between us wordlessly with the arrow-straight silence of spirit entangling with spirit. I cannot tell you what that sweetness of soul, what that light in the mind, what that tenderness in the heart, were like. Only those who have experienced it will understand me here.

Supernaturally, I have prayed and prayed, especially when the sadness—that awful pain of soul—has attacked me and made me wish my life were over, prayed that: "no, Lord Jesus, if You create such a beautiful spirit as You did in my Tati, if You endow her with even the desire to be more than she is by nature, then You cannot—at the cost of Your Own Honor—You cannot let it fall arbitrarily into non-being, into nothingness just because the outer shell, her physical organism oldens, and You, the Lord of Life for little dogs as well as men and angels, decide to withdraw Your Spirit and Your vitalism from her, so that she quit this mortal scene."

I cannot express to you the pain of that sadness when she had died. I cannot tell you what misery it provides. But, in my love for Tati, I kept praying: "Well," I said to my Lord of Life, "little Tati served you well for fifteen years. She gave me an example of daily fidelity, of unswerving devotion, of chaste living, of joy, of happiness. Now You have taken her. Now, therefore, let her render her ultimate service. How?

"Well, I still see her everywhere and at all times. She successfully became identified with every part of my life. So every time I see her in remembrance, at her various places, then I will see You, Blessed Lord. Her remembered presence will become Your remembered presence. I will thus retain her blessed memory, but she will lead me to You. This is surely Tati's ultimate service to You. For she was a source of spiritual benefit to me in a way I never could have imagined before I felt the impact of her being as a feeling entity endowed with an imagination and a memory and, on top of that, a certain clearly defined heredity. She automatically knew so much—and so much no one had taught her."

Chiefly, in the order of the supernatural, her benefiting of me lay in the direction of the goodness of God's world—the goodness intended by the Creator and Father who, on completing His creation, "saw that it was good." My faith and Christ's revelation taught me that there is a specific spiritual difference between Tati and me, a very vital difference lying in the area of free will and intellect as faculties or abilities of my human soul. My terrible (and, at the same time, possibly blessed) ability to love God and say "Yes, I will serve" or alternately to say: "No, I will not serve." From Tati that ability was excluded forever.

Instead, her spirit—in this, like mine and any other sort of spirit—was a dimension of being that could expand or contract according to an outside influence; whereas I was enabled by my creator to be able to resist or accept either expansion or contraction in virtue of my free will and intellect. Tati had not this potential. No free will. No *intellectus agens.* Tati had, instead, the direct intuitive power. She understood directly, immediately, *illico,* without any need for images or ratiocination or deduction or induction. She knew when she made a mistake—we never physically punished her; just *looks* and *words.* She reacted "guilty" and came for forgiveness and re-instatement. Likewise, she sensed when she and I were touching the higher plane, which I am sure she sensed as totally above her, as something she could not touch, a height she could not attain—could only be lifted to it by her father or her Nona.

From experience with her and other dogs, I do believe that there are "good" canine spirits and "bad" canine spirits, that is, certain dogs are born with a negative weight to their spirits paralleling (but not the same as) children born with "bad seed" tendencies; and other dogs are born with a positive gravamen to their spirit which parallels (but is not the same as) children born with "good seed" tendencies. I am using the term "spirit" instead of soul merely out of habit, reserving "soul" for us humans merely to recall the basic distinction between Tati as a spirit and me as a spirit. Because, absolutely certain it is that she and I are more than a physical organism or a merely transitory psychic arrangement of perishable acts and actions. Anyone who has lived, really lived and communed with a dog knows what I'm talking about.

How far the canine spirit can be expanded is the deepest question. No doubt about it, as KL and I noted again and again, if Tati had been treated in a brutal and brutalizing way, it would have brought out all the really "animal" instincts of a terrier bent on survival. We were careful to make her know we were displeased when she started baring her teeth nastily. We did this, not by physical punishment, but by voice and look. Tati responded to that sort of admonition: the incipient nastiness would disappear, her ears and tail would register her regret, her submission, her love; she wanted to grovel in her peculiar way, to be taken up and held, to lick your cheeks and mouth, obviously seeking forgiveness and re-instatement. Which of course none of us could deny her, on the spot!

The expansion of her spirit, the humanization of her spirit, went very far and, in typical canine fashion, by intuitive leaps and unevenly, so that she conveyed to me—again in short bursts of realization—an entire outlook on creation and animals and man and the cosmos. This change in me—it was a real change—was effected by no part of my 18-year Scholastic training by Jesuit trainers, nor by all I read and learned and experienced.

I had to wait for this little dog endowed with this intuitive communicating power to enter my life, so that my adult and supposedly sophisticated world became obviously peopled by angels and babies and I heard constantly the whole hymn of creation which, as St Paul preached, was and is in gestation for deliverance by the Word of God made flesh. Christ did say: "It is consummated." Yes, His sacrifice was. But the working out of that consummation through the intricacies of creation—that takes as long as the age which God the Creator has set for creation's life and ultimate termination when all will be consumed in the Final Unveiling of His divinity.

Only by living with this little dog was I introduced *in re* to this reality about which my trainers and masters and directors had explained the details *theoretically.*

Thus, under her influence—particularly around the time of my morning Mass—I formed in my spiritual life a totally new alliance of little friends and advocates and heavenly patrons. Of course, the sanctifying grace of His Body and Blood and divinity brought it about.

There were concrete factors, too, used by Jesus. There must have been a combination of Tati's behavior towards babies, plus the very distressing effect the Rescue Movement had on me, plus the overall deterioration of the Child as such in U. S. A. life, plus the innovation in my Mass of prayer for aborted ones and Baptismal prayers for them.

But bit by bit, little soul by little soul, I began to include a whole team of departed babies in my morning prayers which by that time consisted mainly of the Nine Angelical Salutations.

Thus, with Tati around my feet, I spoke (and still do speak) personally with the Angels of All Nine Choirs invoking for each choir the holy names of those babies—my angelic brothers and sisters: little Jim Martin, Baby Livanos, Baby Vernicos, Baby Catherine and Daniel FitzMaurice, Baby James Quentin Margand, Baby Teresa Ann Campo Pearson, Baby Denise Zuppe, Baby Julianne Densen-Gerber, Baby Lucadamo, Baby John Augustine Karls, Baby Christina

Holt, Anthony and Denise and Marie La Ferfara. Some were aborted by men. Some were aborted by natural miscarriage. Some, like Ann Campo Pearson were anencephalic and were "terminated." Some, like Christina Holt, were beaten to death by their mother/father/boyfriend. Some like my FitzMaurice ancestors were killed in an accident (in 1876). Some, like Baby Margand, the parents and I asked Our Lady to take home to Heaven because physically their lives would have been miserable; and She did take them gently with a minimum of pain.

But these, through Tati's influence, are now my companions and intercessors; I pray with them; and every day they repeat after me the words of Consecration for the Wine at Mass, because, as I told and instructed them, Jesus loves their voices; and while I as a priest have the Consecratory power, they as innocents and some of them as martyrs, have an entrée with the Divine Majesty that I, a dirty old sinner, cannot have. They're great!

Thus it came about that I had moments of illumination about creation, life, death, the Four Last Things and God's ineffable being and the *investigabiles divitias Christi*. Looming very large on my horizon were two passages from Scripture. One was from the *Apocalypse* (5:11–14) where the Holy Ghost teaches clearly about the participation of little dogs

(among other animals) in the Glory of the Lamb at the final scene of Christ's ultimate triumph:

> "In those days, I heard the voices of many Angels around the Throne, and also of animals, and of the Elders. And their number was in the thousands of thousands, all of them saying in a loud voice: 'The Lamb, because he was killed, is worthy to have attributed to him strength, divinity, honor, glory and blessing.'
>
> Then I heard every creature—those in the skies, those on the surface of the earth, those beneath the earth, those who are on the sea and all in it—I heard them saying: 'To the Lamb sitting on the Throne, let there be blessing, and honor and glory and power for ever and ever.'
>
> And the four animals said: 'Amen.' And the twenty-four Elders fell flat on their faces, and adored the One Who lives for ever."

The second passage is from *Romans* 8:18–23.

> "Brethren: I think that the sufferings we undergo in our present condition are utterly dwarfed by the future glory

> which will be revealed in us. For creatures of God are oriented to the revelation of the Sons of God. Creatures are subjected to this-worldliness, not because they decided that, but because He Who instilled hope in them so decided. For creatures themselves will be liberated from this slavery to corruption, and into the liberty of the glory of the Sons of God. We know that all creatures groan and up to this point are in travail. And not only creatures, but we ourselves who possess the primacy of spirit: we ourselves within ourselves are groaning in our wait for our adoption as Sons of God and the redemption of our body, in Christ Jesus Our Lord."

Those middle years of Tati's life with us were therefore banner years for me in relation to my interior life and the place of the supernatural in my life. In those years, several strands of my life that I had always seen as running—at the best—parallel and—at the worst—in different directions, quietly and without any fanfare came together and were plaited into a pattern which, I know, will be the pattern of my life, of my dying, and of my eternity. I want to indicate those lines and—verbally, at least, pull them together here. The whole point of doing this is to tell you why I said that nobody ever did and could ever love me the way Tati did.

The earliest sounds in my life—and I have some very clear memories of life before I could walk upright—were sounds, first of all, sounds of seagulls circling around Ballylongford, circling and crying that lonely kind of call that is not really lonely; and secondly the sound of the waves. Ballylongford was on the Kerry coast of the Atlantic; we always had in the distance a very dim persistent susurro of ocean water. Barely walking, I was taken with my siblings to Beal (the "Mouth" in Gaelic) where we children (four boys and one girl, Netta) ran mother naked in the sun. The earliest sight I remember was the huge harvest of leaves golden, yellow, purple, brown being swept around Bayview House (our home) by the winds of Autumn which sang and sang and sang, never viciously, always lulling, always keening, always reminding; and the second most vivid memory is Mass in St Michael's parish church where we were all baptized, and specifically of that golden yellow light Father Allmann, the priest, took from the Tabernacle and gave to my parents when they knelt at the Communion Rail. It was a lovely light. I can still see it in my memory's eye.

When I grew up and was educated, at a certain middle stage of my Jesuit training it became almost an obsession for me to find Christ's beauty in the beautiful things of nature. Not of people. Of nature. It was the time they had me studying the Humanities, Greek, Latin, Hebrew, Aramaic, etc. But it never quite all came together at that time. Chiefly because I was so underdeveloped supernaturally, I was in the grip of prejudices—Irish nationalism, a provincial outlook on men and women, no true perception of the difference between culture and civilization. I say "chiefly" because now it seems to me there was a built-in difficulty arising from my Jesuit training.

When I entered the Jesuit Novitiate in Emo, Co. Leix, Ireland, on September 8, 1939, the aim set before us as aspirant Jesuits was to be *socii Jesu,* companions of Jesus in the *Campañia*, the Society, of Jesus. Ignatius was, after all, a soldier. The prime quality of a *socius Jesu* was total devotion—body and soul—to Jesus. That meant no devotion to any other cause, to any other human being in themselves. The Jesuit was supposed to be "detached" in his likes and dislikes; all sensual and worldly beauty, no matter how legitimate and how pure, had to be subordinated to that unique and exclusive attachment to Jesus. This led to the concept of "indifference." The ideal seemed to be: if one was indifferent to praise or to blame, to comfort or the lack of it, under the control of no emotion that could evoke a response from us, but staying steadily and sturdily independent of all human vagaries. This was the ideal.

Of course, strictly speaking, this was and is the ideal. The Church in multiple ways harps continually, in Mass prayers, on this point: it's the *terrena despicere, sed caelestia amare.* True. So true. So perfect. Our only mistake was thinking that just because we knew this and realized this mentally, then in some way or other it was already an accomplished fact. The sequel of course was to last almost fifty years, in my case anyway, and eventually began to achieve that ideal *in re*—to some degree—only because of the intrusion of a little dog into my life.

Roughly but fairly accurately speaking, it took me from age 20 to age 70, and fifteen of those years under tutelage from my babies and my Tati, to arrive at knowing what the virtue of chastity is, what the state of celibacy is—a pure and simple gift of the Father specifically through St Joseph, Mary's husband and foster-father of Jesus, and what all my early and middle-age rhapsodizing about esthetic beauty really led to. There's no way I can summarize even in one paragraph or one whole chapter, the mess I made of everything in my search for that beauty and its harmonious symmetry, the sins I committed, the feelings I hurt, the hopes I dashed, the disappointment I evoked, the coldness for those who truly loved me, the selfishness, and the boring failures of my life. Jesus knows it all, has punished me heartily for much of it, but in His mercy, and in His knowledge of my inmost nature, used a little dog to bring me to heel and show me that *in fine finali* all I really wanted all along and now summarily and exclusively want is to be absorbed in the Holy Trinity forever.

And this he did by allowing me to become physically associated with Tati so that I too through her experienced this groaning expectation I share with all creatures, as St Paul teaches, and learned that thanks to the life, death, resurrection and ascension of my

Lord Jesus, I together with all the Elect can attain eternal felicity in the name of Christ the Power of God and Christ the Wisdom of God. I have learnt bitterly, by now willingly, about that horrible defect running zig-zag throughout the whole of creation from top to bottom that turns beauty into ugliness, virtue into vice, perfume into stink, shapeliness into skewness, warmth into cold, life into death, making predators out of all animals, making cruelty a condition of survival, the shedding of blood and the destruction of life the condition for some to live on.

It is a strange result of my Lord's very loving and planned education of me that I can now pray that prayer of Vesting sincerely: "Let me be able to wear the maniple of sorrow and pain so that I will receive the reward for labor in exaltation," *mercedem laboris.* I no longer have negative thoughts about Adam and Eve—I used to have—because I now realize that the *stola immortalitatis* I lost in the *praevaricatione primi parentis* has been won for me through suffering and obloquy, His suffering and His obloquy.

The mystery of it all is that this consciousness and realization of what genuine (not text-book) indifference really means, that this has come to me through such hardship, so many vile sins and iniquities, and in the company of a Cairn Terrier. Prepare to laugh at me (not sardonically but sympathetically) when I assert that now, only now, after all the *strages* of a useless life, *now* I am ready to be a genuine Jesuit, a real live honest-to-God *socius Jesu.* If I could start all over again now I could rival Peter Canisius or Peter Faber or even Lainez or at least some of those early companions of Ignatius. Please laugh with the Angels at this, and then pass on quickly to pray for my soul—its purification in my short remaining time and its ascent to God's arms the day He calls me home forever.

But perhaps now you can see that no new dog could take Tati's place, and why I say she gave me a love that no one else did or could or will give me.

Into these considerations, you must add the following one which I assure you is of great weight in deciding the direction of my will.

Daddy gave me a red-haired Irish terrier when I was fourteen. A little pup. He was mine. I called him Teddy. He lived outside the whole year round in his own kennel. He was a good watchdog, chained up during the day, roaming the yard and garden and property at night. Teddy, I now know, loved me, looked to me as his master. But I was incapable of responding. He did succeed in conveying his needs—and that was my first concrete experience of intuitive relationship with a dog. He did it simply: standing in front of me staring at me, he sort of held my gaze and suddenly I knew what he needed—e.g., to renew all the straw in his kennel, some fresh water, to pick a pebble out that had got caught between his claws, whatever. But I was incapable of loving him. Besides, I was preparing, as of age 16, to enter the Jesuits.

My chief spiritual activity—inner or interior activity in my last two years before entering the Jesuits—was based on a book called *GOD WITHIN US* by Raoul Plus S. J. It molded my mode of prayer mightily. Of course, I went through reams of vocal prayers to a galaxy of saints, and we all went to Mass and Communion every morning at 7 a.m. winter and summer.

But my interior prayer followed a definite pattern: some power fused around my soul—sightless, soundless, but sweet and peaceful beyond telling. Gradually, a desire arose in me for what I couldn't formulate (I was spiritually illiterate) and the desire hurt. The power came over my soul at no regular times. The last clear time before I entered the Jesuits in 1939 was in our library. I had gone to get down an encyclopedia. That power fused all over me again but this time with an inner vision. I heard myself say interiorly: "Please, give me all of this joy." And then a voice that filled me with wonder said—again soundlessly but absolutely clearly: "Yes, but wait." It all may sound banal. It wasn't, believe me.

Once I entered the Jesuits, of course I left Teddy at home. Apparently he went into decline. When my parents were allowed to see me for the first time after a couple of months, they brought Teddy along. On arrival, they tethered him to the bumper of the car and came in to see me. When I heard Teddy was there, I went out by myself and looked at him. He looked at me, wagged his tail a few times then squatted down, put his head between his paws and looked up at me. I knew what he was saying to me: You left me; you never really knew me: you never really loved me. I know that. You don't know it yet. You will. It will be too late for you and me. But it won't be too late for you. I'm closed out. You no longer want my attachment to you. All that he conveyed to me by his studied collapse and by that intuitive look. But only years later—fifty years later—did Tati teach me to admit that I had been incapable of beatifying Teddy, of making him a really human dog. For that is what human love can do for a dog.

But I went on blithely, unknowingly. After passing through the usual asceticism of the Novitiate's beginnings, the Master of Novices, John Neary (now in Heaven), decided to put me on a special reading and meditation course. In particular he gave me a very famous book by the French Jesuit Grandmaison. It was the life of Consummata, a French mystic who died in 1918 or 1921. But the way Christ treated her interiorly was a very striking parallel with how he was treating me. Consummata became a heavenly patron of mine, and she figures every day with my babies and my angels in my prayers.

There was a dip in all that interior life until I was picked out of a line by old Fr McInerney five years later. He introduced me to the writings of John of the Cross and, from then on, I knew I had been given the inner doctrine of prayer which I needed. But again, in spite of all that, in spite of my *understanding* the mechanics and the process whereby the soul can—if God so wills—escape the traps of the senses, can pass into the Dark Night of the soul, nothing really advanced. My sins and infidelities multiplied. The *Sturm und Drang* of life itself at Louvain, in Rome and New York battened about me and taught me that only reality as devised by Christ could bring me onwards and save me from sinking into the old Slough of Despond and Inertia Bunyon describes. That reality was neatly incarnated in Tati and the entire texture of her life.

The last summer, 1995, and then the autumn and winter were very hard on Tati. Her trachea, already weak from birth, collapsed, so that she had to breathe through an aperture no bigger than the diameter of a needle. She suffered. She could not bark except by exceptional effort. For fully six months, she went around the house heaving and breathing heavily. I besought the Lord Jesus to ally her sufferings with those of all humanity and of all creation which, as St Paul teaches, is groaning in painful expectation of a Redeemer who would heal the Original Defect and restore creation to its original and intended godliness.

Then suddenly, all the heavy breathing stopped, she went off her food, just drank a little water. KL said: "This may be the end." It wasn't. She resumed eating again, but in a much weaker state. The end was near.

One year previously I had made the acquaintance of Charles Cotterill of New Jersey, his wife Sylvia, and his two children, Camillo and Cassandra. Sylvia is mainland Chinese, both children are Taiwanese and adopted. They are now Americans, but they know and love their parents who could not have given them any sort of life. Camillo is a computer expert, Cassandra is going to be a teacher. Charles is British and a mathematician and physicist. He has leukemia. Their pet dog Cricket died of cancer; Charles asked me to help the family bury him.

We all went out to the Peaceable Kingdom (PK), the loveliest pet cemetery in the

Continental U. S. A. It's out in Hartsdale, Westchester, New York. When you enter the PK and stroll down the hillside (it's on the banks of the Hudson with Manhattan towers just a skyline in the distance), you know immediately that everyone buried here is at peace, that all are here because they were *loved*, they aren't here because somebody had to get rid of their remains. It is so well-named: the Peaceable Kingdom. It could just as aptly be called: the Kingdom of Loved Ones. Only love brought each one here who lies sleeping in their Creator's land.

That August of 1995, Charles drove me out to PK, and I purchased a plot for Tati, in addition to a little casket for her. Charles took the casket home to his house; he had space; and KL, I knew, couldn't stand the idea of keeping a casket (even for a little beloved dog) in the basement storage. Tati's plot is in a quiet corner, under the shade of young trees and surrounded by other little dogs. I contracted for perpetual care for her grave and in time I will erect a little tombstone.

In those last months of Tati's life, August '95–March '96, the association of my heavenly babies, her constant desire for "talking tours" and "moaning" sessions, her constant insistence to lie at my door, her eyes fixed on my face as I worked at my desk, the obvious imminence of her dying, and my recurrence to those two passages of Scripture, all this of course made communication with KL and Genie impossible on the subject of Tati's demise. They could not talk about that. Their defense against the imminent sorrow of losing her was: "She's an old dog." "She has to go." When Genie touched on the demise of her own beloved dog, Pembo, she made no bones about it: she would have her "put down" at the end and cremated and she was not concerned further about the remains, etc. I repeat: this was their defense against the pain of separation.

Quite obviously, I could not do that to Tati. If I were to do that, I would dishonor myself. I could not live with myself. I had to bury Tati in the expectation of that liberation which all the Sons of God—His creatures—will undergo when Christ completes the redemption of this cosmos, when He heals that ugly defect distorting His originally "good" creation, and when eternity begins.

KL had one other exigency: Tati would not be allowed to die at home; she would have to die in the Park Avenue Animal Hospital. Only Christ in His gentleness and omnipotent providence was able to arrange so that Tati would come to die naturally and there was a doctor available to certify her death and the PK were available for a burial service—all this on one particular day, March 16. Tied in with this articulation of diverse events was my confiding of Tati's health to St Joseph whose Solemnity, as you know, we celebrate on March 19 every year. That ikon of my life, brother Liam, a great devotee of St Joseph, died a day or two before the 19th in 1981. You can always rely on St Joseph. He is the foster father of all of us. In life and in death.

That hot stinky summer and autumn of 1995 were a little hell for Tati, according as her trachea collapsed and the medicine became less and less efficacious. There was a change in Tati, and I could not communicate it to KL or Genie or anyone else. She wanted much more "talking tours," and she took to taking a siesta on my bed preceded or followed by a "moaning session"; after I had spoken of Heaven and the Angels and "all our babies," she would nestle her head beneath the edge of the pillows and go to sleep. Also she started "looking" at me. This she had started before but sporadically. It is the same way the Angels use when they want to alert me to an ongoing mistake of mine or to something I must do or have omitted to do. They just "look" at me. I cannot say in words what this means. But it amounts to this: I know what is to be done just as if someone spoke it in words, but I have no memory of the words they used or the *sound* of a voice—the quality of the voice, eyes, but not the sound, and I am as certain

of the message as if they had used a bullhorn or spoken through a mini-microphone stuck in my ear. So with Tati. When we ate dinner, she would "look" at me telling me what she needed. When I came into a room where she was, and if she "looked" at me, I would know. When I was at Mass or at my table, the same process would go on. But only at this time did she perfect it, as if it were her last attempt to be what I always described her as to friends, "a human dog," not a dog-dog. There was a second crisis in early February: she went off food, threw up everything, lost control sporadically of her elimination process; she was terribly ashamed of all that and tried to hide her face from me. When I tried to kiss her, she turned her head away—actually she was bringing up a lot of acid and had a rim of saliva around her mouth. I wiped this away and then she would consent to lick me briefly. But, in her "look," she told me she knew she was heading for the big transition and she just wanted to fall asleep near me.

In the last ten days, in the early morning and during the afternoon sessions, after the "talking tour" and the "moaning" conversations, before she fell asleep, there were moments of illumination when it all fell into place. I reread to her that passage from the *Apocalypse* (5:11–14) where the Holy Ghost teaches clearly about the participation of little dogs (together with all good animals) in the Glory of the Lamb at the final scene of Christ's triumph and the elevation of all us "Sons of God."

But Christ Our Lord took her life-forces away so gently, so gradually, that without any prolonged agony, slowly but surely and in a matter of one week, He shut down all the psycho-physical systems that made her organism go; her hearing was more and more impaired, so that noises startled her. The cataract in her right eye grew more acute, and her vision began to lose any definition, so that she had to move her head in order to focus. Then the blood tests showed her kidneys suddenly gone out, her pancreas stopped functioning. Her legs started to give way, and for the first time she started collapsing in mid-stride. She drank only spoonfuls of water, took no food, and was afraid of licking my face or hands because of the acidic taste in her mouth. She slept a good deal and wanted to be beside me or in view of KL.

All of this gathered up so that on Saturday March 16, she had started to die in the real sense of the words. KL said goodbye to her in the den. I took her in my arms over to the Park East Animal Hospital accompanied by Charles Cotterill and Cassandra Cotterill. There, as God would have it, it was Dr Lisciandro who helped give her a tranquilizer. But it was all typical of Tati.

She lay on a blanket on the table. Around her were Charles, Cassandra, George (a hospital orderly) and Dr Lisciandro. I arranged signals with the Doctor. Tati was just barely with us. She did for one last time raise her head and stared at each one of the others in the face and slowly: Charles, Cassandra, George, Lisciandro, then back at me. I kissed her once more, and she gave me one short last lick. Then the head sank slowly between her paws which I held while my eyes held her eyes. I saw relief mirrored alive in her eyes before all liveliness left those beloved eyes, and was replaced by that mute and glassy stare of death. I know, in that last look around, Tati was looking for two faces, KL's and Genie's.

Her burial was on a sunny day. The Peaceable Kingdom never looked more peaceable. The evergreen trees were waving and soughing in a wind which was cleansing but not paining. The grave had been dug. We uncovered the casket before lowering it in. Tati looked so tranquil that it was difficult not to believe she had simply fallen asleep and was ready to wake up at any given moment.

I joined hands with Charles and Cassandra, and I prayed out loud to her Guardian Angel; to my Guardian Angel and my Birthday Angel; then to our Mother Mary Immaculate; and finally to the cause of all our joy on this earth and the sole hope we have of eternal felicity and beatitude, Lord Jesus in His beauty and His power and His wisdom; thanking Him for taking her before me and so gently, at that; asking Him to purify me in preparation for my dying day; and assuring Him that Tati's ultimate service to Him—after a life of creaturely service—would be to turn my mind to Him in His Sacramental presence so that when I remembered her, I would remember Him, and when I blessed her memory, I would bless His continual presence in my soul and His Sacramental presence in my daily life. Blessed be her memory! Please say that prayerfully as you end this letter. Say it to Our Lord Jesus.

We threw handfuls of earth on the casket, once lowered; then the three diggers filled in the grave and withdrew. We had brought some fresh flowers for the grave. Charles played some lovely music. I knelt down and said a decade of my Rosary in honor of Our Lady's Assumption.

Just beyond the gravesite, a middle-aged couple were visiting what was obviously the grave of a very beloved pet indicated by a graven tombstone. She, the wife, was weeping quietly, and watched Tati's obsequies. As I stood up, she caught my eye and said through her tears: "This is as good as it gets. It doesn't get any better." Not wanting to disturb her, I bowed to her, unsmiling. He, the husband

LUCY
ALEX
TATIANA

(who had been speaking Italian with her) said: "*Beh! La vita! Sé nasce e sé ne va!*" I could only bow to him also, and say to both "*Addio.*" I meant it in both senses: "farewell," *and* "be with God." For I knew that it does get better—in fact it's going to get so much better at the Resurrection that it gets to be the best possible! And I also knew that man is not only born (*sé nasce*) and then departs in death (*sé ne va*) but he does this because, from the instant of conception to his last breath, he's on the road to Eternity where Love itself has prepared those beauteous mansions. Man is not a passing stranger born by chance and liquidated at random and mercilessly. He is a redeemed soul beloved of Love Itself.

In her last few months of life, when her movements were slow and labored—Tati had had a permanent damage to her right front paw due to the carelessness of a groomer, and another accident had injured her back, and this injury was only made worse by arthritis in her hind paws—I used to carry her from our rooms to the kitchen and back and elsewhere in the house. When somebody asked me if I was bothered by having to carry a little old dog who had grown fat (22 pounds) and whose limbs were no longer supple, I said spontaneously and truthfully: "I love every ounce of this little body. I love carrying her." And I did.

Being picked up was one of the key steps in humanizing Tati: she had a special way of looking at me when, in the middle of a crowd of adults and humans, she needed to be lifted above the level where little dogs must perforce live and operate: the level of human feet. Always they see those feet coming at them everywhere and always. To be held at my chest level and thus look into everybody's face and eyes, and hear their words—very important for Tati—on that level, this was a supreme privilege, which she never abused. Once I did it and she had tasted the privilege, then she struggled and wriggled until I put her down, and she was off to find one of her balls or to drink water or whatever.

In those last weeks, I had watched her carefully, telling myself that shortly, very shortly I would no longer see her here and there and all around her usual haunts because she would have been called home by the Creator and her body would lie buried in that casket at the Peaceable Kingdom. I envisaged being without her, and I found the sadness stark and unremitting in those last weeks.

Now that she has gone home and the PK holds her remains, of course I see here everywhere, here and there and all around, her haunts in the house. For there is not one place I can go and sit or stand in this house where she and I have not been together and played or talked or kept each other silent company. Is that too high a price in sadness to pay? It would be if indeed as that lady said to me: "This is as good as it gets."

But Tati's ultimate service is now in play, her ultimate service to my loving Lord Jesus. Only, it is not so easy to express in a few words; and the chief reason for this is the very nature of the supernatural. Because, if Tati serves my Lord Jesus, it must therefore serve His supernatural process. For His purpose is our sanctification, and our sanctification means our being slowly but surely assimilated to the life of the Holy Trinity, while we still are mortal. This assimilation is effected by sanctifying grace—that marvelous entity by which I am gratuitously elevated to the status of the Sons of God. Therein lies the whole difficulty of expressing Tati's ultimate service.

For there is no essential connection between any created entity or the whole of creation taken together, no connection between them and God the Creator and His Divine Word. No essential connection. The being of created things and of all creation is the result of a purely gratuitous act of God. He in no way depends on them. He owes them nothing. They have no claim on His supernatural life as a Holy Trinity. Simply the abyss between Him and His creatures is complete.

Christ came to tell us that God had decided to bridge that abyss gratuitously, simply because He is love. And to bridge it completely, so completely that men could truly be called the Sons of God and truly share in the divine life of the Trinity. He not only told us about this. He effected this by His Passion, Death, Resurrection and Ascension.

In Tati's case, as for all other creatures in my life, they either help me to share in this divine life offered me by His grace or they hinder me. Nobody and nothing is really neutral, not when it comes to personal likes and dislikes involving my will. For the Lord Jesus is most jealous about my will. If I am to belong to Him, the intentionality of my will must be oriented directly and (as far as possible) unwaveringly to Him.

The whole purpose of that Jesuit education in *indifference* was precisely to effect that one-way unwavering intentionality of the will. Now it is easy to modify ideas and concepts, to provide oneself with a whole schema, a humanistic schema, according to which one can think about Jesus and God and the Trinity. One can even go further and recast all of nature around us in such humanistic garb. And Manley Hopkins, of course, underlined this so inimitably in a stanza from his *Wreck of the Deutschland*:

I kiss my hand
To the stars, lovely-asunder
Starlight, wafting him out of it...
Kiss my hand to the
  dappled-with-damson west.
Since, tho' he is under the
  world's splendor and wonder,
His mystery must be instressed,
  stressed;
For I greet him the days I meet him,
  and bless when I understand.

Thus the humanist can through ideas and concepts cultivate God's omnipresence. But when it is a matter of *emotions*—love, hate, joy, sadness—above all, sadness!—another agency is needed. For beautiful concepts and ideas cannot effectively bridge that abyss. For, in deep and necessary reality, the supernatural—the Trinitarian life we aspire to share even in this mortal life as well as in the afterlife—that supernatural is *toto caelo* different from an imagined picture, appearance, sight. So different is the supernatural!

The only hope we have—and we have it!—is that He will grant His sanctifying grace so that the stars, the starlight, the dappled-with-damson West, the world's splendor—all and each one can be an occasion for His grace to elevate me, lift me up from between the feet of mortals and allow me to hear His words and see His eyes.

A priori, it would seem that, in being so devoted, so detailedly devoted to Tati, I have stored up for myself an ocean of sadness. Do not speak to me of sadness! I have had private agonies of sadness over Tati's leaving us that I can share with no human being. To share would be desecration. And that is the point of Tati's ultimate service to my beloved Lord Jesus.

Surely I have had this sadness since March 16—you know, the type of sadness which makes you fall asleep because it is the only psychophysical refuge left you after all the prayers and all the spiritual submission. But rapidly my angels and my babies taught me to steer into the sadness, not to run from it: every time and every place she came to mind, they enabled me to turn the stream of sadness straight in Christ's direction. And this is Tati's ultimate service to our common Lord and Master and God: that her very departure becomes for me an occasion of greater devotion, of spiritual Communions, and—most importantly—the development of that holy indifference in me with stricter attachment to the invisible and supernatural, to my hidden God. Verily, Thou art a Hidden God—this was Isaiah's exclamation.

I know, there is that remaining little point, a delicate one. Okay, so Tati—and please God, all created things, but she especially—has become a source of greater and greater assimilation of me to the Holy Trinity. But—here it is!—what about my beloved Tati herself? Is there no possible assimilation of Tati to the Holy Trinity's life? Have I seen the last of my beloved once I blessed her in her casket and covered her body with solid earth? How can Tati share in the ultimate joy of the Sons of God?

I have told Our Lord Jesus and all my angels and babies and the Heavenly Mother of all the Living, Mary, that I cannot—but cannot—even imagine for one moment that my wondrous and adorable God, the *Deus Faber* of Ignatius, the Father who watches over every little sparrow which falls from the housetop, I cannot admit to myself for one instant that, having created something as spiritually beautiful as Tati's spirit, He would dismiss this, utilitarian-wise, and let it tumble into non-being, with nothingness.

I do not know—nor need I know—what my God will do, has already done for my beloved companion Tati who has to the best of her God-given abilities served my Redeemer in me, His priest, and in so many others. Love Incarnate and Goodness personified are flawless. So I live in expectation of the final Resurrection and of seeing Tati with all of glorified creation gathered around the awesome throne of my God's divine majesty. No more tears. No more loneliness. No more solitary sadness. But just joy.

Now forgive the prolixity of this which set out to be a letter of simple explanation. But I owe it to you and to Tati and, we can suppose, to Our Lord and Savior, to tell of the little modest obscure but consoling wonders He does accomplish far from the prying and irreverent eyes of this unhappy, godless world.

—Blessings and much affection,

Printed in Great Britain
by Amazon